Sedimentary Rocks

by Ruth Owen

Consultant: E. Calvin Alexander Jr., Professor Emeritus
Earth & Environmental Sciences
University of Minnesota, Minneapolis

BEARPORT
PUBLISHING

Minneapolis, Minnesota

Credits

Cover and Title Page, © Checubus/Shutterstock; 3, © Silver Spiral Arts/Shutterstock; 5T, © Tatiana Gordievskaia/Shutterstock; 5M, © Vyacheslav Svetlichnyy/Shutterstock; 5B, © Laurie K/Shutterstock; 7, © Simon Greig/Shutterstock; 9, © daniilphotos/Shutterstock; 10, © Shutterstock; 13, © Leene/Shutterstock; 15, © lialina/Shutterstock; 16, © /Shutterstock; 17T, © Designua/Shutterstock; 17B, © YegoroV/Shutterstock; 19T, © Joaquin Corbalan P/Shutterstock; 19B, © jannoon028/Shutterstock; 21, © iacomino FRiMAGES/Shutterstock; 23T, © MaryDesy/Shutterstock; 23B, © rybarmarekk/Shutterstock; 25, © Anton_Ivanov/Shutterstock; 26, © Michele Vacchiano/Shutterstock; 27, © Keneva Photography/Shutterstock; 28, © VectorMine/Shutterstock.

President: Jen Jenson
Director of Product Development: Spencer Brinker
Senior Editor: Allison Juda
Associate Editor: Charly Haley
Designer: Colin O'Dea

Library of Congress Cataloging-in-Publication Data

Names: Owen, Ruth, 1967– author.
Title: Sedimentary rocks / by Ruth Owen.
Description: Silvertip books. | Minneapolis, Minnesota : Bearport
   Publishing Company, [2022] | Series: Earth science - geology: need to
   know | Includes bibliographical references and index.
Identifiers: LCCN 2021026690 (print) | LCCN 2021026691 (ebook) | ISBN
   9781636915814 (library binding) | ISBN 9781636915883 (paperback) | ISBN
   9781636915951 (ebook)
Subjects: LCSH: Sedimentary rocks–Juvenile literature.
Classification: LCC QE471 .O94 2022 (print) | LCC QE471 (ebook) | DDC
   552/.5–dc23
LC record available at https://lccn.loc.gov/2021026690
LC ebook record available at https://lccn.loc.gov/2021026691

For more information, write to Bearport Publishing, 5357 Penn Avenue South, Minneapolis, MN 55419. Printed in the United States of America.

Contents

Everyday Rocks

What do chalk and coal have in common? They are both made of **sedimentary** (sed-uh-MEN-tur-ee) rock. Even pills for upset stomachs are made with this kind of rock! Sedimentary rocks can do many different things. But they all form in the same ways.

There are three kinds of rocks. They are sedimentary, **igneous** (IG-nee-uhs), and **metamorphic** (met-uh-MOR-fik). Rocks are grouped based on how they form.

It All Begins with Sediment

All sedimentary rocks are made of smaller rock pieces. These pieces are called **sediment**. Sediment comes in different sizes. The pieces can be as large as soccer balls. They can be as small as dust.

Look closely at a handful of sand. The pieces of sand are tiny rocks. Sand is sediment!

Sediment can be different colors and shapes.

The Journey of Sediment

Sediments start as parts of bigger rocks. They may be from rocks as large mountains. Over time, small pieces break off from the bigger rocks. This can happen when something brushes against the rock, such as a rushing river flowing down a mountain.

Any kind of rock can be broken into sediment. Igneous, sedimentary, or metamorphic rocks may all become part of new sedimentary rocks.

The pieces eventually come together somewhere. A river may carry a mountain's sediment into a lake or ocean. Then, the sediment sinks down to the bottom of the water. Over thousands of years, new sediment gathers on top of the old. **Layer** upon layer of sediment builds up.

Layers of sediment

When rain, snow, ice, or wind breaks up rock, it is called weathering. And when the sediments are carried by water, wind, or ice to new places, it is called **erosion** (ee-RO-zhun).

Making Rock

The layers of sediment are heavy. Over time, they become pressed together. This forms sedimentary rock.

Sedimentary rock often forms underwater. When the water dries up, the rock can be seen. All of this happens over millions of years!

Many sedimentary rocks have stripes. That is because the layers can be made of different kinds of sediments. The stripes show sediments that are different colors.

What's in Sediment?

Almost all rocks are made of **minerals**. This includes the rocky sediments that make up sedimentary rocks. Sandstone is a sedimentary rock made mostly of a mineral called quartz. The tiny pieces of quartz are stuck together by even smaller bits of other minerals.

Some rocks are made of sediments that are bigger than tomato seeds. Other minerals hold the pieces together.

Conglomerate (ken-GLOM-ur-it) is a sedimentary rock with large sediments.

From Living Things

Some sedimentary rocks come from things that were once alive. One of these rocks is coal. Millions of years ago, plants died and fell into water. Then, the dead plants were buried under sediment. As the sediment turned to rock, the plants did, too. They became coal.

Like coal, chalk is a sedimentary rock made from living things. It has the shells of tiny ocean animals.

How Coal Forms

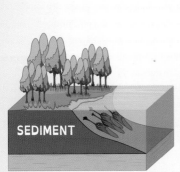

SEDIMENT

SEDIMENT

DEAD PLANTS

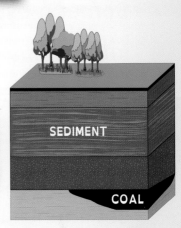

SEDIMENT

COAL

MILLONS OF YEARS

Coal

Sometimes, buried plants do not turn into sedimentary rock. They can become **fossils** held in sedimentary rock. Fossils come from dead plants or animals buried in sediment. As the sediment slowly turns to rock, the dead things can become fossils inside the rock. Sedimentary rock may hold fossils of bones, teeth, and leaves.

Millions of years ago, the Ocucaje Desert in Peru was covered in water. How do we know? The sedimentary rock there has fossils of water animals.

Animal fossil

Plant fossil

Changing Shape

Sedimentary rock can be formed into amazing shapes. And these shapes slowly change over time. The Wave is a large curved rock. Long ago, flowing water made this shape in sedimentary rock. Now, the water has dried up. But the Wave's shape continues to change with weathering from wind.

After wind breaks off tiny pieces of the Wave, those pieces get blown to new places. One day, they might become new sedimentary rock.

The Wave is in a desert in Arizona.

In Utah, water and ice have helped shape tall rocks called hoodoos. Rain and melted snow can drip into cracks in the rock. When the weather gets cold enough, that water turns to ice and gets bigger. The ice pushes open the cracks in the rock, and rock pieces break off. This changes the shape of the hoodoos.

The rock that falls from the hoodoos becomes new sediment. Sometimes, these pieces are as big as vans. They break into smaller pieces on the ground.

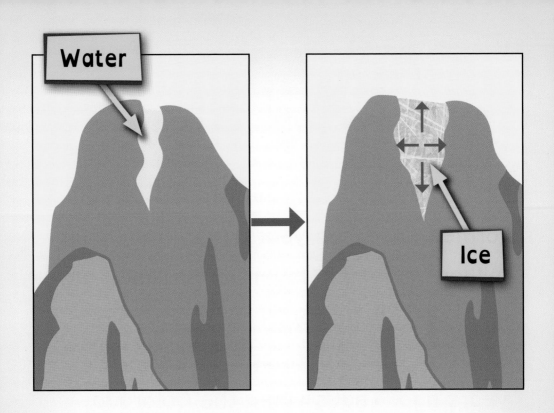

Water

Ice

Weathering from rain also changes the shape of hoodoos.

A Grand History

The oldest rocks in the Grand **Canyon** formed 1.7 billion years ago. Then, over millions of years, layers of sedimentary rock built up on top. The area became dry, rocky land until about 5 million years ago. That's when the Colorado River began to flow over the land. Slowly, it washed away some of the rock and made the canyon.

Today, the Colorado River is still changing the shape of the canyon. In the future, the river may dry up. But the rocky land will continue to change.

The Grand Canyon

With the canyon cut into the rock, the layers can be seen. They look like stripes. These layers help show us Earth's rocky history. Sedimentary rock can tell us what Earth was like when each layer formed long ago.

The Grand Canyon was once covered in water. How do we know? Its rock holds fossils of small sea creatures!

FOLLOW ALONG WITH
Sedimentary Rock

Rain falls on a mountain. It breaks off sediment.

The rain washes the sediment into a lake.

Over thousands of years, layers of sediment build up.

The layers press together into sedimentary rock.

★ SilverTips for REVIEW

Review what you've learned. Use the text to help you.

Define key terms

erosion   sediment
layers   weathering
minerals

Check for understanding

What are the three different kinds of rocks?

Describe two ways that rock can be broken into sediment. What is the same about these ways and what is different?

How can water help make sedimentary rocks?

Think deeper

What can people learn from studying sedimentary rocks? Why do they matter?

★ SilverTips on TEST-TAKING

- **Make a study plan.** Ask your teacher what the test is going to cover. Then, set aside time to study a little bit every day.

- **Read all the questions carefully.** Be sure you know what is being asked.

- **Skip any questions** you don't know how to answer right away. Mark them and come back later if you have time.

Glossary

canyon a steep valley carved out by a river

erosion the breaking off and carrying away of sediment from rocks

fossils the remains of plants or animals that lived long ago

igneous one of the three main types of rock that forms from magma or lava that has cooled and become solid

layer a level of something, such as rocks, lying on top of or under another level

metamorphic one of the three main types of rock that forms when rock changes from one type to another because of heat or pressure

minerals solid substances found in nature that make up rocks

sediment tiny pieces of rock that have broken away from larger rocks

sedimentary one of the three main types of rock that forms from layers of tiny pieces of rock

Read More

Fretland VanVoorst, Jenny. *Sedimentary Rocks (Blastoff! Discovery: Rocks & Minerals).* Minneapolis: Bellwether Media, 2020.

London, Martha. *Grand Canyon (Engineered by Nature).* Minneapolis: Abdo Publishing, 2021.

Pettiford, Rebecca. *Sedimentary Rocks (Geology Genius).* Minneapolis: Jump! 2019.

Learn More Online

1. Go to **www.factsurfer.com** or scan the QR code below.

2. Enter "**Sedimentary Rock**" into the search box.

3. Click on the cover of this book to see a list of websites.

Index

About the Author

Ruth Owen has written hundreds of non-fiction books. She lives on the rocky Cornish coast in England and has always been fascinated by rocks.